All is Well

the unending blessing
of what is

Author's Note

Enlightened teachers insist enlightenment isn't about finding the solution to a complicated problem.

They say it's just a matter of acknowledging the obvious.

When these teachers experience their great realizations, they smile.

They smile at the conspicuous nature of their discoveries, as if the truth is hidden in plain sight.

And they smile at the ridiculous nature of their previous search.

So, what did these teachers discover?

This book is an attempt to answer this question, insofar as the answer can be put into words.

1. I Am

I Am what "I" have sought.

I Am the changeless,
unfathomable One.

I Am Love - infinite and
undying.

I Am that which alone exists.

I Am the brilliant darkness,
and I Am the untroubled
depths.

I Am the dreamer of the
world-dream, and I Am the
unfathomable which exists
beyond dreams.

I Am pure freedom - how wonderful!

It's all Me, but I Am never lonely.

Infinite Love, Infinite Peace and Infinite Bliss always shine in my Heart.

2. Manifestation

I Am like a soap bubble.

My iridescent surface seems
to teem with possibility – as if
there are infinite forms.

Like the glass beads in a
kaleidoscope, there's a play
of possibility.

Touch the kaleidoscope
lightly and it forms new
patterns, but always with the
same glass beads.

It's all Consciousness
knowing itself.

It's all Love loving itself.

Now it appears as a
meadow, now a mountain.

Now a stranger, now my
dearest friend.

The iridescence flowing over
a soap bubble's surface is in
the eye of the beholder only.

It's an innocent play of
manifestation.

Light refracts through a
transparent surface and the
eye interprets red, blue and
green.

I seem to identify with one of these forms, but there is no separate identity.

The flow can't separate itself from itself.

3. Will

*If I'm not a separate person
with free will, how will I attain
enlightenment?*

What if the spoke of a wheel
imagined it was separate and
had "free will?"

What if it thought it was
freewheeling?

Absurd!

Like the spoke of a wheel,
you have no free will, and no
separate desire or feeling.

The personal body and
mind?

The body-mind will do what it
can't not do.

The apparent suffering of
others?

The body-mind will always
help where it can.

You'll do what you'll do.

The mind will think thoughts.

The thoughts will get the
body to do what it would
have done anyway.

That's as far as it goes.

14

An appearance – a
movement of fantasy.

4. The World

*If I'm lost in appearance,
then how do I seek the real
world?*

How you lament an innocent
dream!

You don't have to "wake up"
from your dream to the clear
light - it's here.

In what light do you think this
appears?

Your unfathomable essence
likes to strut around like a
peacock, that's all.

17

We call this manifestation
"the world."

5. The Light of Truth

In the light of Truth, what should I do?

Just remember nothing is wrong and nothing has the power to make anything wrong.

Believe in the truth you know in your heart: nothing can ever go wrong.

If you experience your dream as a nightmare, it's only because you're exploring constriction.

19

Meaning, you're exploring the experience of thinking things can go wrong.

Every state can appear – it's perfectly allowable.

Even the state of non-freedom can appear as a natural expression of freedom.

But in truth you are perfectly free.

Don't worry about how things appear.

It's all an innocent manifestation and you can be perfectly at ease.

Everything has been done for you and every problem has been solved.

"You" are just out of a job.

Do you understand?

It's all heaven and it has all been arranged for you, forever.

22

6. Spiritual Practice

How do I support my spiritual practice, so I may realize freedom?

The body-mind is only a spark thrown by the fire of dreams.

Your practice and intention?

What a notion!

But I don't blame you for entertaining the idea.

There seems to be a mechanism at work.

23

You think you'll "learn to meditate," for example, and a meditation hall seems to appear.

When you're ready to give it up, you'll see it was only a burden.

Even your meditation cushion couldn't support you.

You thought it could support you, but you had to drag it around like everything else.

Nothing can hold you.

Your true being is like water and your worldly experience is a sieve.

Seeking enlightenment
assumes you are not
enlightened already.

So, don't seek
enlightenment.

Be as you are.

7. Peace

How do I find peace of mind?

You want to find peace, but
you *are* Peace, pretending to
be a person.

Let yourself dissolve, and
you'll realize you are Peace.

Or, just forget it.

You are infinite peace, so
what does it matter what
attitude you take?

It's all You pretending to be
out *there* again.

27

What can you gain or lose?

The illusion was over ten million years ago.

At the same time, it never began.

Just glory in its passing, like a comet.

Such good fortune!

You're both lover and beloved.

Love loves itself always and it doesn't bother with the form.

There is never any meaning in form.

28

8. Realization

So, what should I do?

You can love unconditionally, which is the only purpose of your apparent existence as a separate self.

You can experience infinite gratitude, called realization.

The personal mind plays with possibilities, but it doesn't know anything.

The "mind" is only a bundle of thoughts.

Cease to identify with
thinking and it will go away
by itself.

Thinking likes to paint itself
into corners of apparent
constriction.

When you see how you're
duped, you will laugh.

You will laugh at your
attempts to free yourself, too!

You'll see you were trying to
free yourself from heaven, so
you could get back to
heaven.

The angels helped you –
what could they do?

30

The angels always help you.

Just know this:

All is well.

God alone exists.

Seeking meaning in objects
is like the sun trying to see
by the light of the moon.

Turn your attention from
objects which reflect the light
to the light itself.

Remain absorbed in infinite
bliss in your heart.

9. Enlightenment

What is the enlightened state?

The Kingdom of God is like a mustard seed.

It's the smallest of seeds, but it grows into a magnificent tree, sheltering the birds of the sky.

The Kingdom of God is the nascent faith that such shelter is ever-available.

Knock, and the door is opened immediately.

Plant the seed, and the tree
is already here.

The trusting ones never
leave the shelter of the tree.

The untrusting endure cycles
of wandering under a pitiless
sun.

The Kingdom of God is like a
buried treasure.

When the trusting stumble
upon it, they sell everything
they have to secure the field
where it's buried.

When the untrusting stumble
upon it, they find they can't
part with their belongings, so

they're unable to purchase
the field.

They grab a few pearls to sell
at the market, and the
treasure is looted, scattered
and lost.

The personal mind grasps
after the images it sees in the
mirror of the world.

Grasping after images is
called desire.

Desire grasps for happiness,
but never secures it.

Grasping for happiness is the
cause of all trouble.

All trouble vanishes when you abide in bliss, in the heart.

When you abide in bliss, the mind, realizing it is out of a job, subsides.

The mind is the trouble, so the mind must subside.

Only bliss remains.

10. The Universe

What is the universe?

The universe is made of
thought alone and it's only an
appearance, like a dream.

The universe doesn't exist in
deep sleep.

Dreams are the development
site of the waking state,
where the mind explores
possibilities.

The universe experienced in
the waking state is like a fruit
stand on a street corner: in

37

the morning it's assembled from the goods in the store, and in the evening, it's disassembled entirely and brought back into the store.

In the same way, the universe is projected by the mind upon waking and vanishes when the mind sleeps.

"You" are just a character in your dream.

Your dream is dynamic and temporal, so you're very busy.

If you think you're a good person, then you're busy reforming the world.

If you think you're a bad person, then you're busy reforming yourself.

The mind is very busy, but the Self does nothing and is perfectly at ease.

11. The Dream

Maybe I'm a character in my own dream.

If so, what should I do?

The question is moot, as the body will do what it does regardless of anything.

The body is like a gold watch that ticks along exactly as designed.

There is nothing wrong with the body so don't disturb it and don't disdain it.

If you want to live in accordance with Truth, let nothing disturb your peace of mind.

Peace of mind comes from knowing only God (or Love) is real.

Only the supreme reality exists, and You are that reality.

Think of it this way:

When you walk to the train, you carry your heavy backpack.

42

When you board the train,
you put your backpack on the
floor between your feet.

The train and you are going
the same way; you are
carried along by the train.

If you want to honor God, put
down your backpack of
decisions and cares.

This is the proper
acknowledgement.

To worry and condemn isn't
proper and it's a terrible
burden.

12. The Basis

The Supreme Self is the
basis of the universe, of all
that is seen and unseen.

It is also your soul.

The Supreme Self abides in
its own nature and is
unaffected by the so-called
events of life.

Simply abide in the infinite
bliss of the heart.

Sometimes, it may seem that
bliss "goes away."

Bliss doesn't go anywhere,
but the mind gets distracted
and an apparent universe
arises.

This is called "thinking."

See the universe as nothing
but a projection of thought.

Realize that nothing exists
from its own side, not even
your own body-mind.

See all as bands of a single
rainbow of light.

Know that the clear light
cannot be seen.

Remain still.

Keep silence in your heart.

Then, being no one yourself,
you will love all as your Self.

Printed in Great Britain
by Amazon

38725120R00030